Financial Literacy for Beginners Dealing With Inflation

A Simple Guide to Managing Money, Debt, and Savings When Everything Costs More

Get Out of Credit Card Debt With This Book

Are you tired of living paycheck to paycheck? Drowning in interest rates and minimum payments that never seem to shrink your balance? *Understanding & Overcoming Credit Card Debt* is your roadmap to financial freedom.

https://www.amazon.com/dp/B0F3WCVWG8

Avoid Wasting Money On Crypto With This Book

Whether you're curious, cautious, or ready to invest, this book breaks down complex topics into plain language and cuts through the noise, buzzwords, and get-rich-quick schemes.

https://www.amazon.com/Think-Before-You-Crypto-Understanding-ebook/dp/B0F3YQ1L2Q

How to Sell Gold Jewelry for Cash and Avoid Scams

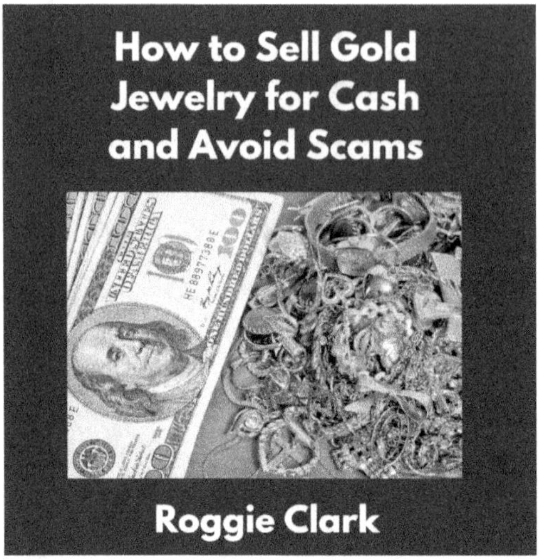

This book was written to help everyday people sell their gold with confidence, protect themselves from common tricks, and get the most money possible.

https://www.amazon.com/Sell-Gold-Jewelry-Avoid-Scams-ebook/dp/B0FW6R6TYN

Copyright

Title: Financial Literacy for Beginners Dealing With Inflation
Author: Roggie Clark

Cover Design: Roggie Clark
Editing: Renee' Clark

Printed in the United States of America

Disclaimer

The views and opinions expressed in this book are those of the author and do not necessarily reflect the official policy or position of any individual, company, or organization cited or referenced in the text.

The author is not affiliated with any of the individuals, companies, or organizations mentioned in the text, nor does the author receive any form of compensation for citing or referencing them. Some sample scenarios in this text are fictitious. Any similarity to actual persons, living or dead, is purely coincidental.

The professional information (strategies, tips, and concepts) in this text is provided on an "as is" basis, without warranties of any kind, express or implied. While every effort has been made to ensure the accuracy of the information contained herein, neither the author nor the publisher makes any representations or warranties regarding its completeness, reliability, or applicability. The information is for educational and informational purposes only and should not be interpreted as professional, legal, financial, or business advice.

This book does **not** constitute financial advice, investment guidance, or legal counsel. Any financial, business, or investment decisions made based on this book are done **at your own risk**. You should always conduct your own research and consult a **certified financial**

advisor, legal professional, or other qualified expert before making any decisions that could impact your finances, business, or legal standing.

Neither the author nor the publisher guarantees any specific results or outcomes. By reading this book, you acknowledge and agree that the author and publisher shall not be held liable for any direct, indirect, incidental, or consequential damages, financial losses, or harm arising from the use or misuse of the information contained in this text. You assume full responsibility for any actions taken based on the content of this book.

Table of Contents

Conclusion

Introduction

One thing that is clear, is that the cost of living today is much higher than it was 10, 20, or even a year ago. The prices of everything including basic necessities such as food, housing, energy, healthcare, etc. have seen a tenfold increase in cost. It looks like inflation maybe the new normal, but it doesn't have to stop your financial progress.

This book was written to close the gap. Inside, you'll learn the fundamentals of financial literacy; how to budget, save, use credit wisely, invest confidently, and protect your money from inflation. In today's fast-changing economy, understanding these skills isn't just helpful,it's essential for stability, independence, and peace of mind when it seems like prices just keep going up.

Whether you're starting from zero or simply want to sharpen your financial knowledge, this book gives you the foundation and clarity to make confident, informed decisions during high inflation times.

Why Financial Literacy Matters Now

We live in an age where money moves fast, costs rise quickly, and financial choices carry more weight than ever. Knowing how to manage your finances is no longer optional; it's a necessity.

Financial literacy isn't about memorizing formulas or mastering technical jargon. It's about understanding how money works, how to make it work for you, and how to protect it from inflation, debt, and poor financial habits.

Whether you're beginning your career, managing household expenses, or planning for long-term goals, informed decision-making determines whether you move forward or fall behind. With rising prices and economic uncertainty, knowledge becomes your most valuable asset.

The Mindset Shift – From Surviving to Building Wealth

I want to make it clear; financial literacy is more than just understanding numbers, it starts with a mindset shift. Moving from simply surviving paycheck to paycheck to actively building wealth requires recognizing that money is a tool, not a source of stress or limitation. This perspective transforms your approach to earning, spending, saving, and investing.

Many people operate on autopilot with money, making reactive decisions based on immediate needs or emotional impulses. Shifting your mindset means planning intentionally, setting clear financial goals, and prioritizing actions that lead to long-term stability and growth, this is truly the key to overcoming inflation. It's about taking responsibility for your financial future rather than relying on luck or external circumstances.

So to be clear, when we talk about building financial literacy, we are talking about making yourself more aware, and resilient during trying economic times.

This mindset shift also involves understanding trade-offs. Every financial decision carries opportunity costs, choosing to spend now may mean sacrificing growth later, while investing today can compound into significant rewards. Recognizing these trade-offs encourages discipline and purposeful decision-making.

But, by adopting a mindset focused on building wealth, you set the stage for all the concepts in this book. Budgeting, saving, investing, and protecting your money become not just tasks but strategic actions aligned with your long-term goals. This mental framework ensures that the lessons you learn are applied effectively and sustainably.

How to Use This Book

With that said, this book is a practical, step-by-step guide for beginners who want to understand and control their finances and overcome inflation. Each chapter builds on the last, moving from the basics of budgeting and saving to debt management, investing, and long-term financial planning. You don't need prior experience—only the willingness to learn and apply what you read.

Approach this book actively. Take notes, review your spending habits, set clear goals, and put the strategies into action. Real progress happens when knowledge turns into behavior. The examples are realistic and grounded in everyday life, so you can apply them no matter your income or background.

By the time you reach the final chapter, you'll have a clear roadmap to manage your finances with confidence, protect your money from inflation, and build lasting financial stability. Financial literacy isn't a one-time achievement—it's a lifelong skill, and this book gives you the framework to master it.

Last Thoughts

Financial literacy matters more now than ever. Understanding how inflation and your financial decisions interact is the key to staying ahead instead of falling behind. The tools and concepts in this book are designed to help you act with confidence, intention, and clarity.

The first step is simple: start. By applying what you learn and staying consistent, you're building the foundation for long-term security, independence, and financial freedom.

Chapter 1: Understanding Your Money

Before you can manage money effectively, you have to understand it. This chapter breaks down what financial literacy really means and why it's the foundation of everything that follows; budgeting, saving, investing, and building long-term wealth. You'll learn the key principles that shape every financial decision and see how improving your financial knowledge can transform your confidence and control over your money.

The Psychology of Money: How Emotions Shape Spending

Money decisions are rarely purely logical. Emotions play a huge role in how we earn, spend, and save. Fear, pride, insecurity, and even social pressure can influence financial choices, often leading to overspending or avoiding important decisions altogether.

Recognizing the emotional triggers behind your financial behaviors is the first step toward control. For example, many people overspend when stressed, using shopping as a quick mood booster. Others might avoid checking their bank accounts out of fear, leading to late payments or missed opportunities. By identifying these patterns, you can implement strategies to make decisions intentionally rather than reactively. Well, how do you do that you ask? Through building your financial literacy.

What Is Financial Literacy

I talked about why financial literacy is important, but what is it really at its core. At its core, it's the ability to make informed, confident decisions about your money. It's understanding not just what you earn and spend, but how to protect, grow, and leverage it in a way that aligns with your goals.

People often underestimate its importance, thinking money management is intuitive. It's not. Financial literacy is a skill set, and like any skill, it requires knowledge, practice, and discipline.

Being financially literate means knowing the difference between assets and liabilities, understanding interest rates, and recognizing the hidden costs of poor money decisions. For instance, carrying a balance on a high-interest credit card isn't just a temporary inconvenience, it could be a drain that compounds over time. Understanding this simple fact changes how you approach debt, spending, and saving.

It's also about perspective. Financially literate people see money as a tool, not a goal. They understand that your income is limited, your time is finite, and the sooner you start making smart choices, the more options you'll have later.

Consider two individuals: one tracks their spending, saves consistently, and avoids high-interest debt. The other spends impulsively and ignores budgeting. Over time, the first person has security, choices, and leverage; the second person is constantly playing catch-up. That's the practical power of financial literacy.

Income, Expenses, and Net Worth

Some of the most basic financial concepts to learn right away would be Income, Expenses, and Net Worth. Before you can manage money effectively, you have to understand where it comes from and where it goes.

Income is obvious, it's the money you earn through work, investments, or other sources. Expenses are everything you spend money on, from rent and groceries to subscriptions and small daily purchases. The challenge isn't just knowing these numbers; it's being honest about them. Many people underestimate their expenses or overestimate their income, which leads to financial strain.

Net worth is a simple but critical metric: it's your assets minus your liabilities. Assets include cash, investments, property, or anything of value that can be converted to cash. Liabilities are debts or obligations, like loans, credit cards, or unpaid bills. Knowing your net worth isn't just a number—it's a snapshot of your financial health. For example, someone might earn $60,000 a year, but if they carry $50,000 in debt and have only $5,000 in savings, their net worth is negative. This is why understanding net worth matters—it drives the decisions you make about spending, saving, and investing.

The key is not to obsess over the exact numbers every day, but to track them consistently. Even a simple monthly review of income, expenses, and net worth reveals trends: overspending patterns, progress on debt, and growth in savings. This awareness alone shifts behavior. It's not glamorous, but it's effective. Financial control starts with knowledge, and knowledge starts with tracking.

The Basics of Budgeting

With that said, let's also talk about budgeting, this is another basic financial concept that is often misunderstood as a restrictive practice meant to limit your life. It's not.

A budget should be a map for your money. It shows you where your money should go, so that your spending aligns with your priorities rather than chaos or impulse. A basic budget includes categories for essentials, discretionary spending, debt repayment, and savings. The exact categories aren't as important as consistency and honesty in tracking.

Start simple. List your monthly income and fixed expenses—rent, utilities, transportation—and subtract that from your total income. Whatever remains can be allocated to savings, investments, or flexible spending. For instance, if your income is $4,000 per month, and $2,500 goes to fixed costs, you have $1,500 to allocate. Decide consciously: $700 to savings, $500 to discretionary spending, $300 to debt repayment. Every dollar has a job.

Budgeting may also require adjustments. Life is unpredictable: prices rise, emergencies occur, and income fluctuates. The key is **flexibility without losing discipline**. If groceries suddenly increase due to inflation, shift funds from discretionary spending temporarily rather than ignoring the problem. A well-planned budget doesn't restrict—it **protects and empowers** you to make choices intentionally.

Lastly, think of budgeting as a feedback system. It's a tool that tells you what's working and what isn't. Over time, it becomes second nature, and the money that once controlled you becomes a tool that serves your goals.

Last Thoughts

I hope you can see now that Financial literacy should be the foundation for every financial decision you make. Understanding your money, tracking your income and expenses, and grasping the basics of budgeting sets you up for control and confidence.

This chapter laid the groundwork—you now know that financial knowledge isn't optional, it's necessary. Apply these principles consistently, stay aware of how your habits impact your goals, and treat this foundation as the first step in a lifelong journey toward financial independence.

I encourage you to continue to build your financial knowledge, while this book can help you do it—it cannot tell you everything. So use this chapter and this book as the starter fuel to ignite your financial knowledge.

Chapter 2: Inflation and Its Impact

Yes, a solid budget can be the backbone of financial stability, but in order for it to be effective you must fully understand what you are up against. Inflation is real, and it is not just some random phenomenon.

In this chapter, you'll learn more about inflation, what it is, how it affects your money; things like the prices you pay, your savings, and even the interest rates you pay on your loans, credit cards or card notes. Overall this chapter is meant to give you a deeper perspective of this concept, and help you see deeper than what the mainstream media is feeding you.

So simply, the point of this chapter is to further shift your mindset to seeing inflation as a deeper indication of the overall strength of the economy rather than just a unique hindrance.

What Inflation Really Means

Inflation is definitely one of those terms that gets thrown around constantly, but many people don't fully grasp its impact on their daily finances.

At its core, inflation is the rate at which the general level of prices for goods and services rises, eroding purchasing power. Simply put, when inflation is high, the money you have today buys less tomorrow. This is not a theoretical concept—it affects everything from groceries to gas to rent.

How Inflation Affects Your Money

Inflation quietly affects every household. Even small increases in inflation can eat away at your savings and purchasing power. A thousand dollars saved last year buys less today if prices have climbed five percent.

Consider a simple example: if a gallon of milk costs \$3 this year and inflation is 10%, that same gallon will cost \$3.30 next year. That might seem small, but compound this across all your monthly expenses—utilities, groceries, transportation—and the effect on your wallet is significant. Inflation quietly reduces the value of money, which is why understanding it is crucial for anyone trying to manage their finances responsibly.

It's also important to recognize the types of inflation. **Moderate inflation** is normal in a growing economy; it encourages spending and investment. **High inflation** or **hyperinflation**, however, can destabilize financial planning, savings, and debt management.

For a beginner navigating personal finance, the focus should be on understanding how rising prices affect your budget and how to adjust before it becomes a problem.

How Prices Affect Your Daily Life

Again, inflation isn't just an abstract economic statistic—it shows up in your everyday life in ways that feel immediate and sometimes frustrating. Rent increases, grocery bills climbing, higher gas prices, and even subscription services slowly creeping up all contribute to a sense of financial strain. People often overlook small incremental changes, but over time, they add up. This is why budgets must be **dynamic and responsive** rather than static.

For instance, imagine your monthly grocery bill was $400 last year. With just a 7% inflation rate, it now costs $428. That $28 difference may seem minor, but multiply it across 12 months, and you're spending $336 more annually just on groceries. Without adjusting your budget, you'll either have to cut back elsewhere or find yourself dipping into savings. Recognizing these shifts is the first step in preventing inflation from undermining your financial stability.

Inflation also impacts discretionary spending. Things like dining out, entertainment, or new gadgets become more expensive, forcing trade-offs. This can feel restrictive, but it's also an opportunity to prioritize spending and make conscious choices. When you understand the mechanisms of inflation, you gain control rather than reacting impulsively to rising costs.

How Inflation Influences Saving and Investing

Inflation isn't just about spending, it also erodes the value of savings if you're not careful. A dollar saved today is worth less tomorrow if it sits in a standard checking account with no growth.

For example, if your savings account earns 1% interest while inflation is 5%, your money loses value in real terms. This is why inflation must be factored into every financial plan, especially for beginners who may underestimate its long-term effects.

Inflation highlights the importance of **regularly reviewing your financial plan**. Budgets, savings goals, and investment allocations are not "set it and forget it" items. Economic conditions change, and a financially literate person adapts their strategy to preserve value and achieve their goals. Inflation is a fact of life, but with knowledge and action, it doesn't have to derail your financial progress.

How Inflation and Interest Rates Affect You Personally

Like I said, inflation can also affect your ability to secure financing. Again, just to reiterate, inflation erodes purchasing power, meaning the same dollar buys less over time. Interest rates, meanwhile, determine the cost of borrowing and the growth of savings and investments.

Understanding both is essential to protecting and growing your money.

For instance, a savings account earning 1% interest in an environment where inflation is 5% is effectively losing 4% of its purchasing power annually. Conversely, higher interest rates can increase your loan costs, making credit cards, mortgages, or car loans more expensive.

Mortgage rates more specifically, are highly affected by inflation—when inflation is high it prompts the Federal reserve to raise interest rates to combat rising prices. Higher inflation also drives up yields on long-term Treasury bonds, which mortgage rates tend to follow, resulting in more expensive mortgages for new borrowers.

As you can see inflation can be a silent killer. But the key is to be proactive—being proactive means accounting for these forces in your planning. Adjust your savings strategies, seek investment vehicles that outpace inflation, and avoid long-term debt that becomes costly as rates rise.

Even small adjustments—like shifting some cash into higher-yield accounts or investment accounts—can make a significant difference over time.

Understanding how inflation and interest rates affect your finances turns abstract economic concepts into actionable steps. When you plan with these realities in mind, you gain control over your money rather than letting the economy dictate your financial outcomes.

Last Thoughts

Inflation is inevitable, but its impact doesn't have to catch you off guard. By understanding how prices affect your daily life, adjusting budgets proactively, and incorporating strategies to protect your savings, you maintain control over your finances.

Awareness and intentional action transform inflation from a threat into a manageable factor in your financial planning. Keep observing trends, adapting your spending, and protecting your purchasing power.

Chapter 3: Budgeting That Actually Works

Okay, so now that we set the foundation, let's talk more about some strategies to help with inflation. We talked about budgeting a bit earlier, but let's really talk about some ways to do it effectively, especially in this high-inflation era.

Saving money isn't just about stashing cash away—it's about security, discipline, and freedom. This chapter explains why saving matters more than ever in an inflation-driven economy and how to build both short- and long-term savings strategies. You'll learn about emergency funds, define clear savings goals, and how saving could be a consistent habit that strengthens your financial foundation.

Tracking Your Income and Expenses

Before you can create a budget that works, you need a clear picture of where your money comes from and where it goes. We already talked about Income, and Expenses in Chapter 1, but here's the thing—many people underestimate what they spend on daily habits like coffee, subscriptions, or eating out, which quietly drains resources over time. Tracking your spending accurately is the foundation of any successful budget.

Start by recording everything for at least one month. Use a spreadsheet, an app, or even a notebook—whatever you will actually maintain consistently. The key is honesty. Include every expense, no matter how small, from groceries to gasoline to impulse purchases. For example, someone might discover they spend $75 per month on streaming services they rarely use. Identifying these leaks allows you to redirect that money toward savings or debt repayment.

Once you have a complete picture, categorize your expenses. Fixed costs like rent and utilities should be separate from variable costs like groceries or entertainment. This helps you identify areas where you can adjust without feeling deprived. The goal is awareness and control, not restriction. When you know exactly how money flows in and out, budgeting becomes a tool rather than a chore.

Creating a Simple Inflation-Proof Budget

With your income and expenses clearly tracked, it's time to build a budget that can withstand rising prices. The key is simplicity and flexibility. It might be a good idea to allocate funds to essentials, debt repayment, savings, and discretionary spending. For example, if your monthly income is $4,000 and fixed costs total $2,500, you have $1,500 to allocate. You might assign $700 to savings, $500 to discretionary spending, and $300 to additional debt repayment. Each dollar has a purpose.

Like I said in Chapter 2, inflation requires that your budget be adaptable. Prices for groceries, transportation, and utilities may rise unexpectedly. A well-designed budget accounts for these changes by maintaining a buffer in essential categories or adjusting discretionary spending temporarily. For example, if your gas bill rises by $50 this month, you might scale back dining out rather than ignoring the increase or dipping into savings. Flexibility keeps your budget realistic and sustainable.

An inflation-proof budget also focuses on prioritization. Essentials come first, then obligations like debt generally come next, and finally discretionary spending. This ensures that even if costs rise, your most critical financial goals are protected. The simpler your framework, the easier it is to follow consistently, which is far more effective than complex, rigid budgeting methods that fail at the first unexpected expense.

The 50/30/20 Rule and Other Budgeting Systems

Here's a framework for budgeting that many follow, that might be good for you as well. The **50/30/20 rule** is a simple framework for managing money: 50% of your income goes to necessities, 30% to discretionary spending, and 20% to savings or debt repayment. This system provides clarity and balance, helping you prioritize essential expenses while still leaving room for enjoyment and long-term financial goals.

While 50/30/20 works for many, it's not one-size-fits-all. Some people may need to allocate more toward debt repayment, while others may have fluctuating income that requires a more flexible approach. Alternative systems, like *zero-based budgeting*—where every dollar is assigned a purpose—can offer more control and precision for those who want to plan every expense in detail.

The key is consistency. Choosing a framework that aligns with your income, lifestyle, and goals allows you to track spending effectively, make intentional choices, and avoid the stress of living paycheck to paycheck. Over time, these habits create a financial foundation that supports both stability and growth.

Again, budgeting should not be about restriction—it should be about greater control. When you understand where your money is going and why, you gain freedom to make conscious decisions that align with your priorities, whether it's saving for a home, investing, or simply having more flexibility in your daily life.

Cutting Costs Without Sacrificing Quality of Life

Sometimes budgeting is just not enough and you have to cut costs. Cutting costs effectively requires identifying areas where spending doesn't contribute to your priorities or long-term goals. For example, instead of canceling your gym membership, which supports your health, you might swap dining out twice a week for cooking at home. Small changes like this can free up hundreds of dollars annually without reducing your quality of life.

Another approach is to be strategic with purchases. Take advantage of discounts, use cash-back programs, and buy in bulk when it makes sense. For example, buying non-perishable groceries in larger quantities can save money over time, but only if it doesn't result in waste. Similarly, reviewing subscription services and eliminating underused ones provides immediate financial relief with minimal lifestyle impact.

Finally, consider lifestyle adjustments that have long-term benefits. Walking, biking, or using public transportation can reduce commuting costs while improving health. Meal prepping at home saves money and ensures you eat healthier. These choices may feel small, but compounded over months, they significantly strengthen your financial position. Budgeting is not about deprivation; it's about **control, awareness, and smart decision-making**.

Last Thoughts

A budget is not a constraint—it's a tool for empowerment. Tracking income and expenses, prioritizing essentials, and building flexibility into your spending plan give you control and clarity. Remember, the goal is sustainability and adaptability, not perfection. Use your budget as a guide to make intentional decisions, adjust to changes like inflation, and allocate resources toward the goals that matter most to you.

Chapter 4: Spending Wisely

Budgeting means nothing if you do not know how to spend money wisely in the first place. This chapter is all about analyzing your wants and needs and learning how to prioritize your spending to ensure that you are living within your means but also are able to enjoy the things that bring you joy and fulfillment.

Prioritizing Needs vs. Wants

Spending wisely starts with understanding the difference between **needs and wants**. Needs are essentials —housing, food, utilities, transportation—while wants are discretionary items, like entertainment, dining out, or luxury purchases. The key is to meet your needs first, then allocate money to wants without undermining your financial goals.

For example, you may want the latest smartphone, but if your budget is already stretched and you're carrying high-interest debt, this is a want, not a need. Prioritizing needs doesn't mean you can never enjoy discretionary spending; it means being intentional. Allocating a fixed portion of your budget for wants ensures you enjoy life without sacrificing financial stability.

Understanding this distinction is especially critical during inflation. As prices rise, discretionary spending may need to be reduced temporarily to cover essential expenses.

The smarter your approach to prioritization, the less likely you are to fall into debt or compromise savings goals. The principle is simple: **spend deliberately, not reactively**.

Smart Shopping Tips During Inflation

Inflation makes spending decisions more impactful. Every purchase should be evaluated for value and necessity. Smart shopping begins with planning. Compare prices, seek discounts, and consider alternatives before buying. For example, switching to generic grocery brands or buying in bulk can save significant money over time.

Another strategy is to evaluate timing. Many products have predictable seasonal price cycles. Purchasing items when prices are lower—like buying winter clothes in late winter or electronics during sales—reduces costs without sacrificing quality. Similarly, leveraging cashback or reward programs effectively turns routine spending into small financial gains.

Finally, avoid emotional spending. Advertising and social pressure can push you to make purchases that don't align with your financial priorities. Before each non-essential purchase, ask whether it truly adds value to your life or simply satisfies impulse. This mindset shift ensures every dollar works for your goals, not against them.

Avoiding Lifestyle Creep

Lifestyle creep is the gradual increase in spending as your income rises. Many people receive raises or bonuses and immediately expand their discretionary spending, which undermines long-term financial goals. Avoiding this requires intentionality and discipline.

For example, if your income increases by $500 per month, consider allocating a portion to savings or debt repayment rather than spending it all on non-essential items. Even small allocations make a significant difference over time. The goal is to improve your lifestyle strategically, not let spending grow unchecked.

Another way to prevent lifestyle creep is by setting financial boundaries and goals. Decide in advance what your priorities are—whether that's building a six-month emergency fund, paying off debt, or investing—and let these objectives guide spending decisions. By consciously managing lifestyle growth, you maintain financial control and avoid the pitfalls of inflation eroding your progress.

Last Thoughts

Spending wisely is about making intentional choices aligned with your priorities. Distinguishing needs from wants, avoiding lifestyle creep, and shopping strategically allows your money to work for you instead of against you. Conscious spending ensures that rising costs or economic pressures do not derail your financial progress.

Approach every purchase with awareness, and let every dollar serve your long-term goals.

Chapter 5: Managing Debt

Credit and debt can either open doors or lock you into years of financial struggle. This chapter helps you understand how credit really works, how lenders view your credit profile, and how to use it wisely in this inflation era. You'll also learn how to manage existing debt, avoid high-interest traps, and make borrowing a strategic tool instead of a burden. Understanding debt and how it can hinder or help you achieve your goals is a crucial part to making your budget or any other financial plan you create a success.

Understanding Good Debt vs. Bad Debt

Debt often gets a bad reputation, but not all debt is harmful. The key is knowing the difference between **good debt** and **bad debt**. Good debt is used strategically to build long-term value, such as a mortgage on a home, a student loan for a career-boosting degree, or a business loan that generates income. Bad debt, on the other hand, drains your resources without creating value, like high-interest credit cards used for impulsive purchases or loans for depreciating items (think those sneaky buy-now-pay-later agreements).

Many beginners assume all debt is negative and avoid it entirely, but that's not always the smartest approach. Understanding the interest rate, repayment terms, and the purpose of each debt helps you make informed decisions. For example, carrying a low-interest student loan may be far better than accumulating high-interest credit card debt to pay for the same education. The difference lies in **value creation versus value loss**.

Recognizing the type of debt you carry is essential for prioritization. Bad debt should be reduced aggressively, while good debt can be managed strategically. Knowing this distinction allows you to take control rather than feeling overwhelmed or guilty about money decisions you've already made. Debt is a tool, and like any tool, its impact depends on how it's used.

Paying Down Credit Cards and Loans Strategically

High-interest debt is the silent killer of financial progress. Credit cards, payday loans, and certain personal loans carry rates that can quickly outpace income growth. The first step in managing these obligations is **awareness**—know exactly how much you owe, at what interest rates, and the minimum payments required.

From there, develop a repayment strategy. Two popular approaches are the **debt snowball** and **debt avalanche** methods. The debt snowball focuses on paying off the smallest balances first, creating momentum and psychological wins. The debt avalanche prioritizes the highest-interest debt first, which is mathematically more efficient. Either method could work if applied consistently.

For example, if you have three credit cards with balances of $500, $1,200, and $3,000, and interest rates of 18%, 22%, and 15%, choosing the avalanche method means attacking the 22% debt first, minimizing long-term interest paid.

Consistency is critical. Missing payments or making only minimum payments prolongs debt and increases total cost. Consider automating payments to avoid missed deadlines. Even small additional payments, like $20–$50 per month, can reduce interest and shorten repayment time significantly. The goal is to take control and make your debt work for your financial plan, not against it.

Avoiding Debt Traps in High-Inflation Times

Inflation complicates debt management because it can increase living costs while leaving your income relatively static. This is where many people fall into a debt trap: covering everyday expenses with high-interest credit instead of adjusting spending. For example, if groceries and gas rise unexpectedly, using a credit card to cover the gap may seem convenient, but it compounds financial pressure in the long term.

To avoid this, plan for **emergencies and rising costs** by maintaining a buffer within your budget. If you have a small emergency fund, you won't need to rely on high-interest debt when prices spike. Additionally, scrutinize borrowing carefully—loans with variable interest rates can become burdensome during inflationary periods.

Understanding the terms and risks prevents short-term solutions from becoming long-term problems.

Finally, think of debt management as part of a bigger financial strategy. Paying down bad debt, avoiding new high-interest obligations, and maintaining discipline with spending ensures that inflation doesn't erode your financial position. By acting proactively, you turn what could be a stressor into a manageable component of your overall plan. Debt is not the enemy—it's **control and knowledge** that make it manageable.

Your Credit Score: The Five Factors That Determine It

In order to effectively pay off debt, you must also monitor your credit score. Your **credit score** is a numerical snapshot of your financial reliability, and it impacts everything from loan approval to interest rates. It falls within a range from 300 to 850. Higher scores (700 and above) indicate better creditworthiness, while lower scores signal higher risk to lenders.

Knowing your score can help you understand how lenders view you and give you insight into your ability to secure better credit terms in the future. Your credit score typically can be found on your **credit report**—which is a detailed record of your borrowing history, showing how well you've managed credit over time.

You're entitled to a free credit report once a year (every 12 months) from each of the three major credit reporting agencies: **Equifax**, **Experian**, and **TransUnion**. You can visit https://www.annualcreditreport.com/index.action to get this score. Also, it's important to understand that these reports are just estimates, your real credit score or **FICO score** can be found at MyFico at web address: https://www.myfico.com/ or you can find it out when you apply for a credit card or loan, but be aware that these things are a "**hard-pull**" on your credit score so it might go down because of it, so just keep this in mind.

Reviewing your credit report and score is an essential part of assessing your debt situation. In order to do that you must also understand the five key factors that determine it—this can help you better manage your credit proactively.

1. **Payment History (35%)**: Making on-time payments is the most critical factor. Missed or late payments can significantly damage your score.

2. **Credit Utilization (30%)**: This measures how much of your available credit you're using. Keeping utilization below 30% is generally advised to show responsible credit management.

3. **Length of Credit History (15%)**: The longer your credit accounts have been open, the more stable you appear to lenders. Even inactive accounts contribute

to this metric.

4. **Credit Mix (10%)**: A healthy mix of credit types—credit cards, installment loans, and mortgages—demonstrates versatility and reliability.

5. **New Credit Inquiries (10%)**: Applying for too much new credit at once can signal risk to lenders, temporarily lowering your score.

By understanding these factors, you can take targeted actions to improve your credit. Whether it's paying down balances, avoiding unnecessary new accounts, or ensuring consistent on-time payments, each choice directly affects your score and financial opportunities.

Last Thoughts

Debt is a tool, not a trap, when managed intentionally. Recognize good debt versus bad, develop a strategic repayment plan, and avoid high-interest pitfalls, especially during challenging economic periods. Taking control of debt reduces stress, frees up cash flow, and positions you to achieve long-term financial goals. Consistency, discipline, and awareness are the keys to turning debt from a burden into a manageable component of your financial plan.

Chapter 6: Saving Smarter

Once you've built a foundation of financial stability by setting up a budget and creating a plan for how to manage debt, the next step is growing your wealth. One of the simplest ways to do this is through savings. Saving money shouldn't just be about stashing cash away—it should be about security, discipline, and freedom. This chapter explains why saving matters more than ever in an inflation-driven economy and how to build both short- and long-term savings strategies. You'll learn how to define clear savings goals, and make saving a consistent habit that strengthens your financial foundation.

Emergency Funds: What, Why, and How Much

An emergency fund could be your financial safety net, designed to cover unexpected expenses such as car repairs, medical bills, or temporary job loss. Without one, even a minor emergency can quickly become a financial crisis, forcing you into high-interest debt or derailing your budget.The ideal emergency fund **typically covers three to six months of living expenses**, though the exact amount depends on your personal situation, income stability, and financial obligations.

Starting small is better than waiting for the "perfect moment." Even $25 or $50 per week adds up over time. For example, if your essential monthly expenses are

$2,000, putting aside $50 per week will build a $1,000 cushion in five months. That initial buffer provides confidence and prevents panic when life throws a curveball.

Ultimately, an emergency fund is more than just money set aside—it could mean more financial freedom and security. Knowing you can handle unexpected challenges without derailing your progress reduces stress, allows better decision-making, and reinforces long-term financial habits.

Automating Your Savings

Creating an emergency fund does require discipline. Automating contributions each month can ensure you consistently build your reserves without thinking about it. Automating your savings can also remove the need for constant decision-making, making it easier to stay on track and grow your wealth steadily. Automatic transfers from your checking to your savings account ensure that a portion of your income is saved before you have a chance to spend it.

Automation also allows you to take advantage of timing and discipline. For example, scheduling savings to coincide with paydays ensures that you treat savings as a non-negotiable expense, just like rent or utilities. Over time, this creates a reliable pattern of saving that compounds with your budgeting efforts that I talked about in Chapter 3.

Additionally, automating your savings reduces stress and temptation. You won't have to rely on memory, motivation, or self-control every month—your system works silently in the background. It also makes it easier to allocate money toward specific goals, such as an emergency fund, retirement, or large purchases.

Ultimately, automation turns saving from a sporadic choice into a consistent, effortless habit. The combination of regular contributions and compound interest ensures that your money grows steadily, giving you control, security, and flexibility in the long term.

High-Interest Accounts and Inflation-Proof Options

Inflation eats away at savings over time, so keeping money in a standard checking account is not enough. To preserve value, a lot of investors and financial planners recommend **high-yield savings accounts**, **certificates of deposit (CDs)**, or **Treasury Inflation-Protected Securities (TIPS)**. Each option has trade-offs between accessibility, risk, and return, but even modest interest rates can help offset inflation.

For example, if you have $5,000 in a regular savings account at 0.5% interest and inflation is 5%, your real purchasing power declines each year. Moving that money to a high-yield account earning 3% reduces the impact, and TIPS or CDs can further protect your funds. The goal is not to chase massive returns, but to **maintain and protect value** while keeping your funds safe. Also, you should know that there are often penalties and tax implications for early withdrawal of some high-yield accounts—so just keep that in mind.

Diversification within your savings is also wise. Keep a portion easily accessible for short-term emergencies, while allocating a smaller portion to slightly longer-term, higher-yield options. This balances liquidity with growth and ensures you are prepared for both everyday needs and inflationary pressures.

Understanding Compound Interest

If you are going to have savings accounts—you must understand how **Compound Interest** works. Compound interest is one of the most powerful forces in personal finance. Unlike simple interest, which only applies to your initial principal, compound interest earns returns on both the principal and any accumulated interest. Over time, this "interest on interest" effect can dramatically increase your savings and investments, even if you start small.

For example, if you invest $1,000 at a 5% annual return, you'll have $1,050 after one year. The next year, you earn interest not just on the original $1,000, but also on the $50 interest from year one. Over decades, this compounding effect grows exponentially, illustrating why starting early is crucial for long-term wealth.

Understanding compound interest isn't just about numbers—it's about mindset. The sooner you start saving, the more time your money has to grow, and the less you have to save each month to reach the same goal. This principle applies to both investments and debt: compounding can work for you in savings or against you if you carry high-interest debt.

By leveraging compound interest, you turn consistent, disciplined saving into significant financial growth. It's a reminder that small, regular contributions can yield substantial rewards over time, reinforcing the value of patience and long-term planning.

How to Save Consistently Even on a Tight Budget

Saving is not about having extra money—it's about prioritizing. Consistency beats intensity. Even small contributions, made regularly, accumulate into meaningful reserves over time. We We already talked about automating savings, and how it can be one of the simplest ways to succeed

But another strategy is to **reallocate money from cut costs**. For instance, if reducing dining out saves $200 a month, redirect it straight into savings rather than treating it as extra discretionary spending. Similarly, any windfalls—bonuses, tax refunds, or side gig income—should also be partially earmarked for savings to accelerate progress.

Finally, track your progress regularly. Seeing your emergency fund or savings grow—even gradually—reinforces the habit and provides motivation. The mindset shift is key: saving should not be a sacrifice; it is **preparing, protecting, and empowering yourself** against uncertainty. With discipline and intentionality, even tight budgets can generate financial security.

Last Thoughts

Saving is both a habit and a strategy. By building an emergency fund, leveraging high-yield accounts, and automating contributions, you protect yourself against uncertainty and inflation. Small, consistent actions accumulate into meaningful security over time. Prioritize your savings, treat them as non-negotiable, and remember that each dollar set aside today increases your options and resilience tomorrow.

Chapter 7: Protecting Your Future

Financial success doesn't happen by accident—it happens by design. Once you've built a foundation of financial stability, the next step is growing your wealth. This chapter introduces you to the basics of investing in plain language. You'll learn about different investment options—like stocks, bonds, and mutual funds. The goal is to help you make informed choices and start building long-term financial growt

Basics of Investing for Beginners

Investing can feel intimidating, especially for beginners, but it's a crucial step in protecting your financial future. At its core, investing is putting your money to work so it grows over time. Unlike saving, which primarily preserves value, investing has the potential to outpace inflation and build wealth. Stocks, bonds, mutual funds, and ETFs are common options, each with varying levels of risk and return. Also, many people invest in commodities like gold and silver, which can provide a hedge against inflation and market volatility.

For example, consider two individuals with $5,000 to invest. One leaves it in a regular savings account earning 1% interest; the other invests in a diversified ETF averaging 7% annually. Over ten years, the investor's portfolio could grow substantially faster, demonstrating how even modest returns can compound over time. Past performance does not guarantee future results, so this is just an example not the standard for what to expect. The key for beginners is to **start early, stay consistent, and focus on low-cost, diversified investments** rather than chasing high-risk opportunities.

It's also important to understand your risk tolerance. Higher returns usually come with higher volatility, so balancing growth and stability based on your comfort level and timeline is essential. Beginners should start with simple, diversified strategies, gradually expanding their knowledge and portfolio as confidence grows.

Risk vs. Reward: Understanding Your Tolerance

Investing is a balance between risk and reward. Higher potential returns usually come with higher risk, while safer investments often yield lower returns. Understanding your personal risk tolerance—how much loss you can endure without panic—is essential for making investment decisions that align with your financial goals.

Risk tolerance isn't just about your comfort level; it also considers your timeline and financial obligations. For example, someone saving for retirement decades away can generally afford higher-risk investments, while someone approaching retirement might prioritize stability over growth. Assessing your risk tolerance helps you select investments that match both your emotional comfort and long-term objectives.

To gauge your tolerance, consider hypothetical scenarios: How would you react if your investment dropped 20% in a month? Could you stay the course, or would you sell in panic? Your answers indicate which investment strategies suit you best and prevent impulsive decisions that could derail progress.

By aligning risk with reward, you can make informed choices that maximize growth potential while protecting your financial stability. Knowing your limits allows you to invest confidently, avoid costly mistakes, and stay committed to your long-term plan.

Understanding Retirement Accounts

Retirement planning is one of the most effective ways to safeguard your future. Employer-sponsored accounts like 401(k)s, or individual accounts like IRAs are one of the most common ways seniors prepare for retirement. These types of accounts can provide tax advantages and often include employer matching contributions.

But contrary to popular belief, the money can't just sit there and earn a decent return without some effort—you do need to make sure that you are properly allocating your funds to different mutual funds in your account in order to actually grow any money.

Also, 401k and IRAs do have transaction and management fees, along with compound interest rates, which can reduce the value of your retirement savings over time. So, you should definitely be aware of these fees and rates when choosing a retirement plan.

Inflation-Resistant Investment Strategies

Like I've been saying, inflation erodes purchasing power, which makes protecting your wealth more than just growing it—it requires strategies that **outpace inflation**. Stocks, real estate, commodities, and inflation-protected securities like TIPS can help preserve and grow value over time. Diversification across these assets reduces risk and smooths out volatility, ensuring your portfolio remains resilient.

For example, during periods of rising prices, stocks in companies that can pass costs to consumers often maintain or increase value, whereas cash sitting idle loses purchasing power. Real estate could act as an inflation hedge, as property values and rents tend to rise with prices, but real estate is a high-risk gamble, that shouldn't be taken lightly and is susceptible to volatility especially during high unemployment times, so again keep this in mind.

Beginners should focus on simple, diversified approaches, avoiding speculation or overly complex strategies until they gain experience.

Finally, regular review and adjustment are essential. Economic conditions change, interest rates fluctuate, and personal goals evolve. Protecting your future isn't a "set it and forget it" process—it's **consistent awareness, learning, and action**. By investing thoughtfully, leveraging retirement accounts, and choosing inflation-resistant strategies, beginners can build a secure financial foundation that stands the test of time.

Avoiding Scams, Fraud, and Predatory Lenders

Financial scams and predatory lending practices can quickly erode investment wealth and damage credit. Understanding how to identify and avoid these threats is essential for protecting your money. Scams can range from phishing emails and fake investment opportunities to payday loans with exorbitant interest rates. Predatory lenders often target those in vulnerable financial positions, offering quick cash with hidden fees and impossible repayment terms.

Being vigilant starts with education. Always verify the legitimacy of financial institutions, investment platforms, and lenders before committing money. Check reviews, confirm licenses, and consult trusted resources when evaluating offers. Awareness of common tactics—

pressure to act quickly, promises of guaranteed returns, or complex hidden fees—helps you spot danger before it becomes a problem.

Simple habits can also reduce risk. Avoid sharing sensitive financial information online, use secure banking channels, and regularly monitor accounts for suspicious activity. Building a habit of cautious and informed decision-making prevents falling victim to scams and ensures your money remains under your control.

Ultimately, protecting yourself from fraud and predatory lenders is as much about mindset as it is about knowledge. By staying alert, skeptical, and proactive, you preserve financial security and maintain the integrity of your long-term financial plan.

How to Prepare for Job Loss or Economic Downturns

Economic uncertainty is inevitable, and preparing for job loss or downturns ensures financial resilience. Unexpected events—company layoffs, recessions, or industry shifts—can impact your income and lifestyle and quickly derail even the soundest of budgets. Being proactive allows you to navigate these challenges without derailing your financial progress.

Start by maintaining an emergency fund that can cover three to six months of living expenses. This fund serves as a buffer, giving you time to adjust, find new opportunities, and avoid high-interest debt. Additionally, diversifying income sources, such as part-time work or side projects, can provide supplemental security if your primary income is disrupted.

Financial planning also includes reducing unnecessary expenses and reviewing recurring obligations (I talked about this in Chapter 3). Streamlining your budget, paying down high-interest debt, and postponing non-essential purchases create flexibility to weather financial shocks. Regularly updating your resume, networking, and skill-building further improve employability and reduce stress during transitions.

Preparation isn't just about surviving—it's about maintaining control. By planning for economic uncertainties in advance, you protect your finances, reduce anxiety, and position yourself to recover quickly and continue building wealth despite setbacks.

Last Thoughts

Protecting your future requires planning, knowledge, and action. Start investing early, take advantage of retirement accounts, and choose strategies that outpace inflation. Wealth isn't just about earning—it's about preserving and growing your resources over time.

Consistency, informed decision-making, and long-term thinking turn uncertainty into opportunity and ensure financial security in the years ahead. Job loss happens, so the key is to stay vigilant, only invest in things you can actually see, and prepare for the unexpected like scams or fraud.

Chapter 8: Building Strong Financial Habits

Wealth isn't built overnight—it's built through consistency, smart decisions, and patience. This chapter ties everything together, showing you how to use what you've learned to build long-term financial security and a plan that works for you. You'll explore habits that strengthen your financial health, learn how to adapt as life changes, and avoid the common mistakes that derail most people's progress.

Setting Goals and Tracking Progress

Financial success begins with clear, measurable goals. Without them, money management becomes reactive rather than intentional. Goals should be specific, realistic, and time-bound. For example, instead of saying "I want to save more," define a target: "I will save $5,000 for an emergency fund within 12 months." Specificity creates focus and accountability.

Like I said in Chapter 3, tracking progress is equally important. Use a spreadsheet, app, or simple journal to monitor income, expenses, and savings. For instance, reviewing your budget monthly can reveal overspending patterns or progress toward debt repayment. This habit not only keeps you accountable but also allows you to celebrate milestones, reinforcing positive behavior and motivation.

Another key is breaking larger goals into smaller, manageable steps. Paying off $12,000 in debt might seem overwhelming, but targeting $1,000 at a time creates momentum and confidence. Goals transform abstract intentions into tangible, actionable steps, turning financial literacy into real-world results.

Automating Your Finances

Automation doesn't have to stop at your savings account—automation could be one of the most powerful tools for building strong financial habits overall. Automating savings, bill payments, and investment contributions ensures consistency and reduces the risk of human error or forgetfulness.

Automation also helps avoid late fees and missed payments, which can derail your financial progress. Imagine forgetting a credit card due date: one missed payment can trigger penalties and increase interest. By automating these obligations, you eliminate unnecessary friction and create a system that works **without constant oversight**.

Even discretionary spending can be partially automated. For example, allocate a fixed monthly amount for entertainment or dining out, and once it's gone, you know your budget is maintained. Automation doesn't replace awareness—it reinforces discipline, allowing you to focus on strategic financial decisions rather than day-to-day micromanagement.

Staying Motivated Through Economic Ups and Downs

Building strong financial habits isn't just about systems and automation—like I said in Chapter 1—it's also about mindset. Economic fluctuations, unexpected expenses, and personal setbacks are inevitable. The key is resilience: maintaining discipline and focus regardless of circumstances.

For example, inflation may increase living costs unexpectedly, or a temporary job setback may reduce income. Those with strong financial habits adapt without panic. They adjust budgets, maintain savings contributions where possible, and keep long-term goals in mind. Viewing setbacks as temporary challenges rather than failures preserves momentum and prevents reactive, harmful decisions. Consistency, small wins, and self-reflection are essential. Reviewing progress monthly, celebrating milestones, and learning from mistakes reinforces positive habits.

Over time, these habits compound just like money in a savings account, creating **financial control and stability that lasts a lifetime**. Strong habits are the bridge between knowledge and results—without them, even the best strategies fail.

Revisit and Revise Your Financial Plan Annually

Financial planning should not be a one-time activity—it requires regular review and adjustment. Circumstances change, including income, expenses, goals, and economic conditions. Revisiting your plan annually ensures that your strategies remain aligned with your objectives and that you're taking advantage of new opportunities.

Start by evaluating your progress toward financial goals, checking investments, savings, and debt repayment. Identify areas where you exceeded expectations, fell short, or need adjustment. This reflection helps you make informed decisions for the coming year.

Next, revise your plan based on updated priorities or life changes, such as a new job, family expansion, or unexpected expenses. Adjust budgets, contributions to savings or retirement accounts, and investment allocations as needed to stay on track.

Annual review also reinforces discipline and awareness. By consistently assessing your financial plan, you maintain control over your money, adapt to changes proactively, and continue building toward long-term security and wealth.

Last Thoughts

Strong financial habits turn knowledge into results. Setting goals, planning, tracking progress, automating actions, and maintaining discipline through life's ups and downs ensures you consistently move toward financial independence. Habits compound over time, and with focus and persistence, you gain control, confidence, and resilience. Financial literacy is only powerful when paired with consistent action.

Conclusion

Financial literacy is not a luxury; it is a necessity in this high inflation era. The knowledge and habits you've developed throughout this book are the foundation of control over your financial life.

In this book we went over the basics of financial literacy, and the psychology of money. We also discussed in detail what inflation actually is and how it affects your purchasing power and ability to save.

We also talked about budgeting and spending wisely. Prioritizing needs over wants, avoiding lifestyle creep, and making conscious purchasing decisions ensures your money serves your goals. We also talked about managing debt, and how it is not inherently bad, but it must be managed carefully. Recognizing the difference between good and bad debt, paying down high-interest obligations strategically, and avoiding new financial traps empowers you to keep your money working for you.

Next, we talked about how saving is more than a habit—it is a shield against uncertainty. Building an emergency fund, taking advantage of high-yield accounts, and automating contributions creates a buffer that protects you from financial shocks. Even modest, consistent savings accumulate into meaningful security over time.

Then, we talked about protecting your financial future through investing—which is how your money grows and outpaces inflation. Starting early, focusing on diversified strategies, and leveraging retirement accounts ensures your wealth has the potential to compound over time. Understanding risk, protecting against inflation, and maintaining a long-term perspective allows beginners to navigate investing with confidence, turning what seems complex into manageable action steps.

Lastly, we talked about building strong financial habits and how they are the backbone of financial literacy. Setting clear goals, tracking progress, automating actions, and staying disciplined during economic fluctuations turns knowledge into results. Habits compound over time, just as money compounds in savings and investments.

Ultimately, financial literacy is a journey, not a destination. Each choice you make, each dollar you allocate intentionally, and each habit you maintain reinforces your ability to control your financial future. Start with small, deliberate actions, track progress, adjust when necessary, and keep learning. Mastery does not happen overnight, but incremental steps lead to lasting results.

You now have the tools to act with purpose, avoid common mistakes, and navigate financial challenges confidently. Control over your money is freedom—the freedom to pursue goals, weather uncertainty, and create opportunities. Use these lessons to build a foundation that serves you, not just today, but for decades to come. Financial literacy is power. Use it.

Glossary of Terms

Here's a quick snapshot of some of the most important terms mentioned in the book.

Assets – Anything of value that you own, including cash, investments, property, or other possessions that can generate income or be converted into cash.

Bad Debt – Debt that does not create value and typically carries high interest, such as credit card balances used for non-essential spending.

Budget – A plan for how you allocate your income across expenses, savings, debt repayment, and discretionary spending.

Credit Score – A numerical representation of your creditworthiness, based on your borrowing and repayment history, which lenders use to determine loan eligibility and interest rates.

Debt Avalanche Method – A strategy for paying off debt that focuses on eliminating the highest-interest balances first to minimize total interest paid.

Debt Snowball Method – A debt repayment strategy that prioritizes paying off the smallest balances first to build momentum and motivation.

Discretionary Spending – Non-essential expenses, such as entertainment, dining out, or luxury items, which are flexible and adjustable.

Emergency Fund – Savings set aside specifically for unexpected expenses or financial emergencies, usually covering 3–6 months of essential costs.

Financial Literacy – The ability to understand and effectively manage financial matters, including income, expenses, savings, debt, and investments.

Good Debt – Debt used strategically to build value, such as student loans, mortgages, or business loans that generate income or long-term benefits.

Inflation – The rate at which the general level of prices for goods and services rises, reducing the purchasing power of money over time.

Interest Rate – The percentage charged on borrowed money or earned on savings and investments, usually expressed annually.

Investing – The act of allocating money to assets like stocks, bonds, or real estate with the expectation of generating a return or growing wealth over time.

Liabilities – Financial obligations or debts you owe, such as loans, credit card balances, or unpaid bills.

Net Worth – The difference between your assets and liabilities, representing your overall financial position.

Retirement Accounts – Accounts designed to save for retirement, often with tax advantages, including 401(k)s, IRAs, and similar plans.

Savings Account – A bank account that allows you to store money safely while earning interest, typically offering easy access to funds.

Spending Plan – Another term for a budget, emphasizing intentional allocation of money to meet goals and priorities.

TIPS (Treasury Inflation-Protected Securities) – U.S. government bonds designed to protect against inflation by adjusting principal value with inflation rates.

Variable Expenses – Costs that fluctuate month to month, such as groceries, transportation, utilities, or discretionary spending.

Wealth – The accumulation of valuable resources, including money, assets, and investments, that provides financial security and freedom.

About the Author

Roggie "Raj" Clark is an entrepreneur and a 10-year marketing professional with a proven track record in e-commerce and digital business growth. Having built and managed successful online stores with thousands of sales and consulted for numerous marketing clients, Roggie has mastered the intricacies of online marketing, branding, and consumer behavior. He has also written several popular books on digital marketing, SEO (search engine optimization), and programming (HTML, CSS, and JavaScript).

As a former marketing manager at a fintech company—a role he secured through his own marketing and financial expertise—Roggie gained firsthand experience in financial strategy and wealth-building. This journey inspired him to share insights with amateur investors, helping them save money, make smarter financial decisions, and build long-term wealth. Raj currently lives in Maryland with his sister and niece.

www.ingramcontent.com/pod-product-compliance
Lightning Source LLC
LaVergne TN
LVHW022315200926
848481LV00004B/1350